50 The Best Lemon Dishes

By: Kelly Johnson

Table of Contents

- Lemon Chicken Piccata
- Lemon Garlic Shrimp Pasta
- Lemon Curd Tart
- Lemon Risotto
- Lemon Butter Salmon
- Lemon Poppy Seed Muffins
- Lemon Bars
- Lemonade
- Lemon Coconut Cake
- Lemon Pepper Chicken Wings
- Lemon Asparagus
- Lemon Sorbet
- Lemon Cheesecake
- Lemon Garlic Hummus
- Lemon Meringue Pie
- Lemon Basil Chicken
- Lemon Grilled Vegetables

- Lemon Ricotta Pancakes
- Lemon Ice Cream
- Lemon Fettuccine Alfredo
- Lemon Herb Roasted Chicken
- Lemon Sugar Cookies
- Lemon and Dill Salmon
- Lemon Butter Scallops
- Lemon Zucchini Bread
- Lemon Pepper Salmon
- Lemon Ginger Chicken
- Lemon Cream Cheese Danish
- Lemon and Garlic Roasted Shrimp
- Lemon Pudding
- Lemon Chicken Salad
- Lemon Roasted Potatoes
- Lemon Thyme Grilled Chicken
- Lemon Fluff Pie
- Lemon Maple Roasted Carrots
- Lemon Scones

- Lemon Lush Dessert
- Lemon-Cucumber Salad
- Lemon Shrimp Scampi
- Lemon Baked Cod
- Lemon Almond Cake
- Lemon-Infused Olive Oil Pasta
- Lemon Glazed Donuts
- Lemon Zest Vinaigrette
- Lemon Chia Seed Pudding
- Lemon Tofu Stir Fry
- Lemon-Blueberry Muffins
- Lemon-Poppy Seed Cake
- Lemon Rosemary Roasted Chicken
- Lemon Watermelon Salad

Lemon Chicken Piccata

Ingredients:

- 4 boneless, skinless chicken breasts
- 1/2 cup almond flour
- Salt and pepper to taste
- 2 tbsp olive oil
- 1/4 cup chicken broth
- 1/4 cup fresh lemon juice
- 1 tbsp capers
- 2 tbsp butter
- Fresh parsley for garnish

Instructions:

1. Season the chicken breasts with salt and pepper, then dredge in almond flour.
2. Heat olive oil in a skillet over medium-high heat. Cook the chicken for 4–5 minutes per side, until golden brown and cooked through. Remove from the skillet and set aside.
3. In the same skillet, add chicken broth, lemon juice, and capers. Stir, scraping up any browned bits from the bottom of the pan.
4. Add butter and stir until melted and the sauce thickens slightly.
5. Return chicken to the skillet and spoon the sauce over the top.
6. Garnish with fresh parsley and serve.

Lemon Garlic Shrimp Pasta

Ingredients:

- 1 lb shrimp, peeled and deveined
- 2 tbsp olive oil
- 4 cloves garlic, minced
- 1/4 cup lemon juice
- 1 tsp lemon zest
- 1/2 cup chicken broth
- 1/4 cup heavy cream
- 1 package zucchini noodles (or 4 cups spiralized zucchini)
- Salt and pepper to taste
- Fresh parsley for garnish

Instructions:

1. Heat olive oil in a large skillet over medium-high heat. Add garlic and sauté for 1 minute.

2. Add shrimp and cook for 2-3 minutes per side, until pink and cooked through. Remove shrimp and set aside.

3. In the same skillet, add lemon juice, lemon zest, chicken broth, and heavy cream. Simmer for 3-4 minutes until the sauce thickens slightly.

4. Add zucchini noodles to the skillet and cook for 2-3 minutes until tender.

5. Return shrimp to the skillet, toss everything together, and season with salt and pepper.

6. Garnish with fresh parsley and serve.

Lemon Curd Tart

Ingredients:

- 1 1/2 cups almond flour
- 1/4 cup coconut flour
- 1/4 cup erythritol
- 1/2 tsp vanilla extract
- 1/4 cup butter, melted
- 6 large egg yolks
- 1/2 cup lemon juice
- 1/2 cup erythritol
- 1 tbsp lemon zest
- 1/2 cup butter, cubed

Instructions:

1. Preheat oven to 350°F (175°C).
2. Combine almond flour, coconut flour, erythritol, vanilla extract, and melted butter in a bowl. Press the mixture into the bottom of a tart pan to form the crust.
3. Bake for 10–12 minutes, or until golden brown. Set aside to cool.
4. In a separate bowl, whisk together egg yolks, lemon juice, erythritol, and lemon zest.
5. Cook the mixture in a saucepan over low heat, stirring constantly, until it thickens.

6. Remove from heat and stir in cubed butter until smooth.

7. Pour the lemon curd into the cooled tart crust and refrigerate for at least 2 hours before serving.

Lemon Risotto

Ingredients:

- 1 cup cauliflower rice (or 1 cup arborio rice for traditional risotto)
- 2 tbsp olive oil
- 1/2 cup onion, diced
- 3/4 cup dry white wine (optional)
- 2 cups chicken broth
- 1/4 cup heavy cream
- 1/4 cup Parmesan cheese, grated
- 1/4 cup fresh lemon juice
- 1 tbsp lemon zest
- Salt and pepper to taste

Instructions:

1. Heat olive oil in a large skillet over medium heat. Add onion and sauté for 2–3 minutes until softened.
2. Add cauliflower rice (or traditional arborio rice) and cook for 1–2 minutes.
3. Add wine (if using) and cook until most of the liquid evaporates.
4. Gradually add chicken broth, 1/4 cup at a time, stirring frequently until the rice absorbs the liquid.
5. Once the rice is tender, stir in heavy cream, Parmesan cheese, lemon juice, and lemon zest.

6. Season with salt and pepper to taste.

7. Serve hot, garnished with more Parmesan cheese.

Lemon Butter Salmon

Ingredients:

- 4 salmon fillets
- 2 tbsp olive oil
- 2 tbsp butter, melted
- 2 tbsp fresh lemon juice
- 1 tsp lemon zest
- Salt and pepper to taste
- Fresh parsley for garnish

Instructions:

1. Preheat oven to 375°F (190°C).
2. Place salmon fillets on a baking sheet lined with parchment paper.
3. Drizzle with olive oil, melted butter, lemon juice, and lemon zest.
4. Season with salt and pepper.
5. Bake for 12–15 minutes, or until the salmon is cooked through and flakes easily.
6. Garnish with fresh parsley and serve.

Lemon Poppy Seed Muffins

Ingredients:

- 1 1/2 cups almond flour
- 1/4 cup erythritol
- 2 tsp poppy seeds
- 1/2 tsp baking powder
- 1/4 tsp baking soda
- 1/4 tsp salt
- 3 large eggs
- 1/4 cup lemon juice
- 1/4 cup melted butter
- 1 tsp lemon zest
- 1 tsp vanilla extract

Instructions:

1. Preheat oven to 350°F (175°C).
2. In a bowl, mix almond flour, erythritol, poppy seeds, baking powder, baking soda, and salt.
3. In another bowl, whisk together eggs, lemon juice, melted butter, lemon zest, and vanilla extract.
4. Combine the wet and dry ingredients until smooth.

5. Pour the batter into muffin tins lined with paper liners.

6. Bake for 18–20 minutes, or until a toothpick inserted comes out clean.

7. Let cool before serving.

Lemon Bars

Ingredients:

- 1 1/2 cups almond flour
- 1/4 cup coconut flour
- 1/4 cup erythritol
- 1/4 cup melted butter
- 1 1/2 cups fresh lemon juice
- 4 large eggs
- 1/2 cup erythritol
- 1 tsp lemon zest
- Pinch of salt

Instructions:

1. Preheat oven to 350°F (175°C).
2. Combine almond flour, coconut flour, erythritol, and melted butter to form the crust. Press into the bottom of a baking dish.
3. Bake for 10–12 minutes, or until golden brown.
4. In a separate bowl, whisk together lemon juice, eggs, erythritol, lemon zest, and salt.
5. Pour the lemon mixture over the baked crust and bake for 20–25 minutes, or until set.
6. Let cool completely before cutting into bars.

Lemonade

Ingredients:

- 1 1/2 cups fresh lemon juice
- 1/4 cup erythritol (or more to taste)
- 4 cups cold water
- Ice cubes

Instructions:

1. In a pitcher, combine fresh lemon juice and erythritol, stirring until the sweetener dissolves.
2. Add cold water and stir well.
3. Taste and adjust sweetness if necessary.
4. Serve over ice cubes.

Lemon Coconut Cake

Ingredients:

- 1 1/2 cups almond flour
- 1/4 cup coconut flour
- 1/2 cup erythritol
- 1 tsp baking powder
- 1/4 tsp salt
- 3 large eggs
- 1/4 cup coconut oil, melted
- 1/4 cup lemon juice
- 1 tbsp lemon zest
- 1/2 cup shredded unsweetened coconut

Instructions:

1. Preheat oven to 350°F (175°C).
2. In a bowl, mix almond flour, coconut flour, erythritol, baking powder, and salt.
3. In another bowl, whisk together eggs, coconut oil, lemon juice, and lemon zest.
4. Combine wet and dry ingredients until smooth.
5. Fold in shredded coconut.
6. Pour the batter into a greased cake pan and bake for 25–30 minutes, or until a toothpick comes out clean.

7. Let cool before serving.

Lemon Pepper Chicken Wings

Ingredients:

- 10–12 chicken wings
- 2 tbsp olive oil
- 1 tbsp lemon zest
- 1 tbsp lemon juice
- 1 tsp garlic powder
- 1/2 tsp black pepper
- Salt to taste
- Fresh parsley for garnish

Instructions:

1. Preheat oven to 400°F (200°C).
2. Pat the chicken wings dry with paper towels.
3. In a bowl, toss the wings with olive oil, lemon zest, lemon juice, garlic powder, black pepper, and salt.
4. Arrange the wings in a single layer on a baking sheet.
5. Bake for 25–30 minutes, flipping halfway through, until crispy and golden brown.
6. Garnish with fresh parsley and serve.

Lemon Asparagus

Ingredients:

- 1 bunch asparagus, trimmed
- 2 tbsp olive oil
- 1 tbsp fresh lemon juice
- 1 tsp lemon zest
- Salt and pepper to taste
- Fresh parsley for garnish

Instructions:

1. Preheat oven to 400°F (200°C).
2. Toss the asparagus with olive oil, lemon juice, lemon zest, salt, and pepper.
3. Spread the asparagus evenly on a baking sheet.
4. Roast for 12–15 minutes, until tender and slightly crispy.
5. Garnish with fresh parsley and serve.

Lemon Sorbet

Ingredients:

- 1 1/2 cups fresh lemon juice
- 1/4 cup erythritol (or preferred sweetener)
- 2 cups cold water
- Zest of 1 lemon

Instructions:

1. In a mixing bowl, combine lemon juice, erythritol, cold water, and lemon zest. Stir until the sweetener is dissolved.
2. Pour the mixture into an ice cream maker and churn according to the manufacturer's instructions.
3. Once the sorbet reaches the desired consistency, transfer to a container and freeze for 1–2 hours.
4. Serve chilled.

Lemon Cheesecake

Ingredients:

- 1 1/2 cups almond flour
- 1/4 cup erythritol
- 1/4 cup butter, melted
- 2 cups cream cheese, softened
- 1/2 cup sour cream
- 1/4 cup erythritol
- 2 large eggs
- 2 tbsp lemon juice
- 1 tbsp lemon zest
- 1 tsp vanilla extract

Instructions:

1. Preheat oven to 325°F (165°C).
2. In a bowl, mix almond flour, erythritol, and melted butter until it forms a dough. Press the mixture into the bottom of a springform pan to form the crust.
3. Bake the crust for 10 minutes, then set aside to cool.
4. In a mixing bowl, combine cream cheese, sour cream, erythritol, eggs, lemon juice, lemon zest, and vanilla extract. Blend until smooth.
5. Pour the filling onto the cooled crust and bake for 45–50 minutes, or until set.

6. Let cool, then refrigerate for 2–3 hours before serving.

Lemon Garlic Hummus

Ingredients:

- 1 cup cauliflower florets, steamed
- 2 tbsp tahini
- 1 clove garlic, minced
- 2 tbsp fresh lemon juice
- 2 tbsp olive oil
- 1/2 tsp cumin
- Salt and pepper to taste
- Lemon zest for garnish

Instructions:

1. In a food processor, combine steamed cauliflower, tahini, garlic, lemon juice, olive oil, cumin, salt, and pepper. Blend until smooth.
2. Adjust seasoning to taste.
3. Transfer to a serving bowl and garnish with lemon zest.
4. Serve with veggies or keto-friendly crackers.

Lemon Meringue Pie

Ingredients:

- 1 1/2 cups almond flour
- 1/4 cup erythritol
- 1/4 cup butter, melted
- 1 1/2 cups fresh lemon juice
- 1/2 cup erythritol
- 4 large egg yolks
- 1 cup heavy cream
- 4 large egg whites
- 1/2 tsp cream of tartar

Instructions:

1. Preheat oven to 350°F (175°C).
2. Combine almond flour, erythritol, and melted butter to form a crust. Press into a pie dish.
3. Bake for 10–12 minutes until golden brown. Set aside to cool.
4. In a saucepan, whisk together lemon juice, erythritol, and egg yolks. Cook over medium heat until thickened.
5. Remove from heat and stir in heavy cream. Pour the filling into the cooled crust.
6. In a separate bowl, beat egg whites with cream of tartar until stiff peaks form.

7. Spread the meringue over the lemon filling.

8. Bake for 10–12 minutes, until the meringue is golden.

9. Let cool, then refrigerate for at least 2 hours before serving.

Lemon Basil Chicken

Ingredients:

- 4 boneless, skinless chicken breasts
- 2 tbsp olive oil
- 2 tbsp fresh lemon juice
- 1 tbsp lemon zest
- 1/4 cup fresh basil, chopped
- Salt and pepper to taste

Instructions:

1. Heat olive oil in a skillet over medium-high heat.
2. Season the chicken breasts with salt and pepper.
3. Cook the chicken for 5–7 minutes per side until golden brown and cooked through.
4. Add lemon juice, lemon zest, and fresh basil to the skillet.
5. Toss the chicken in the lemon-basil mixture and cook for another 1–2 minutes.
6. Serve immediately.

Lemon Grilled Vegetables

Ingredients:

- 1 zucchini, sliced
- 1 red bell pepper, sliced
- 1 yellow bell pepper, sliced
- 1 red onion, sliced
- 2 tbsp olive oil
- 2 tbsp fresh lemon juice
- 1 tsp lemon zest
- Salt and pepper to taste

Instructions:

1. Preheat grill to medium-high heat.
2. In a bowl, toss vegetables with olive oil, lemon juice, lemon zest, salt, and pepper.
3. Grill vegetables for 5–7 minutes, turning occasionally, until tender and slightly charred.
4. Serve immediately.

Lemon Ricotta Pancakes

Ingredients:

- 1 cup ricotta cheese
- 4 large eggs
- 1/4 cup almond flour
- 2 tbsp erythritol
- 1 tsp lemon zest
- 1 tbsp fresh lemon juice
- 1/2 tsp baking powder
- Butter for cooking

Instructions:

1. In a bowl, combine ricotta cheese, eggs, almond flour, erythritol, lemon zest, lemon juice, and baking powder. Stir until smooth.
2. Heat a pan over medium heat and melt a little butter.
3. Pour small amounts of the batter into the pan to form pancakes.
4. Cook for 2–3 minutes per side, until golden brown.
5. Serve with keto-friendly syrup or fresh berries.

Lemon Ice Cream

Ingredients:

- 2 cups heavy cream
- 1 cup unsweetened almond milk
- 1/2 cup erythritol (or preferred sweetener)
- 2 tbsp fresh lemon juice
- 1 tbsp lemon zest
- 1 tsp vanilla extract

Instructions:

1. In a bowl, whisk together heavy cream, almond milk, erythritol, lemon juice, lemon zest, and vanilla extract until smooth and the sweetener dissolves.
2. Pour the mixture into an ice cream maker and churn according to the manufacturer's instructions.
3. Once thickened, transfer to an airtight container and freeze for 2–3 hours.
4. Serve chilled.

Lemon Fettuccine Alfredo

Ingredients:

- 2 cups zucchini noodles (or shirataki noodles for lower carb)
- 1 tbsp olive oil
- 1/2 cup heavy cream
- 1/4 cup Parmesan cheese, grated
- 2 tbsp fresh lemon juice
- 1 tsp lemon zest
- 1 clove garlic, minced
- Salt and pepper to taste
- Fresh parsley for garnish

Instructions:

1. Heat olive oil in a pan over medium heat. Add garlic and sauté for 1–2 minutes.
2. Add heavy cream, Parmesan, lemon juice, and lemon zest. Stir and cook for 2–3 minutes until the sauce thickens.
3. Toss the zucchini noodles in the sauce until well-coated and heated through.
4. Season with salt and pepper to taste.
5. Garnish with fresh parsley and serve.

Lemon Herb Roasted Chicken

Ingredients:

- 1 whole chicken (about 4 lbs)
- 2 tbsp olive oil
- 2 tbsp fresh lemon juice
- 1 tbsp lemon zest
- 4 cloves garlic, minced
- 1 tbsp fresh rosemary, chopped
- 1 tbsp fresh thyme, chopped
- Salt and pepper to taste

Instructions:

1. Preheat oven to 375°F (190°C).
2. In a small bowl, combine olive oil, lemon juice, lemon zest, garlic, rosemary, thyme, salt, and pepper.
3. Rub the mixture all over the chicken.
4. Place the chicken in a roasting pan and roast for 1–1.5 hours, or until the internal temperature reaches 165°F (75°C) and the skin is golden and crispy.
5. Let rest for 10 minutes before carving and serving.

Lemon Sugar Cookies

Ingredients:

- 2 cups almond flour
- 1/2 cup erythritol (or sweetener of choice)
- 1/4 cup unsalted butter, softened
- 1 large egg
- 2 tbsp fresh lemon juice
- 1 tsp lemon zest
- 1/2 tsp baking soda
- Pinch of salt

Instructions:

1. Preheat oven to 350°F (175°C).
2. In a bowl, mix almond flour, erythritol, baking soda, and salt.
3. Add butter, egg, lemon juice, and lemon zest. Stir until a dough forms.
4. Roll the dough into small balls and place them on a baking sheet lined with parchment paper.
5. Flatten each ball with a fork, then bake for 8–10 minutes until golden.
6. Let cool before serving.

Lemon and Dill Salmon

Ingredients:

- 4 salmon fillets
- 2 tbsp olive oil
- 1 tbsp fresh lemon juice
- 1 tbsp lemon zest
- 1 tbsp fresh dill, chopped
- Salt and pepper to taste

Instructions:

1. Preheat oven to 375°F (190°C).
2. Place the salmon fillets on a baking sheet lined with parchment paper.
3. Drizzle with olive oil, lemon juice, and lemon zest.
4. Sprinkle with fresh dill, salt, and pepper.
5. Bake for 12–15 minutes, until the salmon is cooked through and flakes easily with a fork.
6. Serve immediately.

Lemon Butter Scallops

Ingredients:

- 1 lb scallops, patted dry
- 2 tbsp butter
- 2 tbsp fresh lemon juice
- 1 tsp lemon zest
- 2 cloves garlic, minced
- Salt and pepper to taste
- Fresh parsley for garnish

Instructions:

1. Heat butter in a skillet over medium-high heat.
2. Season scallops with salt and pepper and add to the skillet. Cook for 2–3 minutes per side, until golden brown and cooked through.
3. Add garlic, lemon juice, and lemon zest to the skillet and stir.
4. Cook for 1–2 minutes, until the sauce thickens slightly.
5. Garnish with fresh parsley and serve.

Lemon Zucchini Bread

Ingredients:

- 2 cups almond flour
- 1/4 cup erythritol
- 1 tsp baking soda
- 1/4 tsp salt
- 1/2 tsp cinnamon
- 3 large eggs
- 1/4 cup butter, melted
- 1/4 cup fresh lemon juice
- 1 tbsp lemon zest
- 1 cup zucchini, grated and excess moisture squeezed out

Instructions:

1. Preheat oven to 350°F (175°C).
2. In a bowl, mix almond flour, erythritol, baking soda, salt, and cinnamon.
3. In another bowl, whisk together eggs, melted butter, lemon juice, and lemon zest.
4. Add the wet ingredients to the dry ingredients and stir until combined.
5. Fold in grated zucchini.
6. Pour the batter into a greased loaf pan and bake for 40–45 minutes, or until a toothpick inserted comes out clean.

7. Let cool before slicing and serving.

Lemon Pepper Salmon

Ingredients:

- 4 salmon fillets
- 2 tbsp olive oil
- 1 tbsp lemon juice
- 1 tbsp lemon zest
- 1 tsp black pepper
- Salt to taste

Instructions:

1. Preheat oven to 375°F (190°C).
2. Place the salmon fillets on a baking sheet.
3. Drizzle with olive oil, lemon juice, and lemon zest.
4. Sprinkle with black pepper and salt.
5. Bake for 12–15 minutes, or until the salmon is cooked through and flakes easily.
6. Serve immediately.

Lemon Ginger Chicken

Ingredients:

- 4 boneless, skinless chicken breasts
- 2 tbsp olive oil
- 2 tbsp fresh lemon juice
- 1 tbsp fresh ginger, grated
- 1 tsp lemon zest
- 2 cloves garlic, minced
- Salt and pepper to taste

Instructions:

1. In a bowl, combine olive oil, lemon juice, grated ginger, lemon zest, garlic, salt, and pepper.
2. Marinate the chicken breasts in the mixture for at least 30 minutes.
3. Heat a skillet over medium-high heat and cook the chicken for 6–7 minutes per side, or until fully cooked and golden brown.
4. Serve immediately.

Lemon Cream Cheese Danish

Ingredients:

- 8 oz cream cheese, softened
- 2 tbsp butter, softened
- 1/4 cup almond flour
- 1/4 cup coconut flour
- 1/4 cup erythritol (or sweetener of choice)
- 1 large egg
- 1 tsp vanilla extract
- 1 tbsp lemon zest
- 1 tbsp fresh lemon juice
- 1/4 cup powdered erythritol (for topping)

Instructions:

1. Preheat oven to 350°F (175°C).
2. In a bowl, combine almond flour, coconut flour, erythritol, and salt. Add egg, butter, and vanilla extract, and mix until smooth.
3. Roll the dough into a rectangle on parchment paper.
4. In a separate bowl, mix cream cheese, lemon zest, lemon juice, and powdered erythritol until smooth.
5. Spread the cream cheese mixture over the dough, then fold the edges over to create a "danish" shape.

6. Bake for 15-20 minutes, or until golden.

7. Let cool slightly before serving.

Lemon and Garlic Roasted Shrimp

Ingredients:

- 1 lb large shrimp, peeled and deveined
- 2 tbsp olive oil
- 3 cloves garlic, minced
- 2 tbsp fresh lemon juice
- 1 tsp lemon zest
- Salt and pepper to taste
- Fresh parsley for garnish

Instructions:

1. Preheat oven to 400°F (200°C).
2. In a bowl, toss shrimp with olive oil, garlic, lemon juice, lemon zest, salt, and pepper.
3. Arrange the shrimp in a single layer on a baking sheet.
4. Roast for 8–10 minutes, until shrimp are cooked through and pink.
5. Garnish with fresh parsley and serve.

Lemon Pudding

Ingredients:

- 2 cups heavy cream
- 1/4 cup erythritol (or sweetener of choice)
- 3 large egg yolks
- 1/4 cup fresh lemon juice
- 2 tbsp lemon zest
- 1 tsp vanilla extract

Instructions:

1. In a saucepan, heat heavy cream and erythritol over medium heat until it begins to simmer.
2. In a bowl, whisk together egg yolks, lemon juice, and lemon zest.
3. Slowly pour the hot cream into the egg mixture while whisking continuously to temper the eggs.
4. Pour the mixture back into the saucepan and cook over low heat until thickened.
5. Remove from heat and stir in vanilla extract.
6. Pour into serving dishes and refrigerate for at least 2 hours before serving.

Lemon Chicken Salad

Ingredients:

- 2 cups cooked chicken breast, shredded
- 1/4 cup mayonnaise
- 2 tbsp fresh lemon juice
- 1 tbsp lemon zest
- 1 tbsp Dijon mustard
- 1/4 cup celery, diced
- Salt and pepper to taste

Instructions:

1. In a bowl, combine shredded chicken, mayonnaise, lemon juice, lemon zest, Dijon mustard, and celery.
2. Mix well and season with salt and pepper.
3. Serve chilled on lettuce leaves or as a sandwich on keto bread.

Lemon Roasted Potatoes

Ingredients:

- 1 lb baby potatoes, halved
- 2 tbsp olive oil
- 1 tbsp fresh lemon juice
- 1 tsp lemon zest
- 2 cloves garlic, minced
- 1 tsp dried thyme
- Salt and pepper to taste

Instructions:

1. Preheat oven to 425°F (220°C).
2. In a bowl, toss the potatoes with olive oil, lemon juice, lemon zest, garlic, thyme, salt, and pepper.
3. Spread the potatoes on a baking sheet in a single layer.
4. Roast for 25–30 minutes, flipping halfway through, until golden and tender.
5. Serve hot.

Lemon Thyme Grilled Chicken

Ingredients:

- 4 boneless, skinless chicken breasts
- 2 tbsp olive oil
- 2 tbsp fresh lemon juice
- 1 tbsp lemon zest
- 2 cloves garlic, minced
- 1 tbsp fresh thyme, chopped
- Salt and pepper to taste

Instructions:

1. Preheat the grill to medium-high heat.
2. In a bowl, combine olive oil, lemon juice, lemon zest, garlic, thyme, salt, and pepper.
3. Coat the chicken breasts with the marinade and let sit for at least 30 minutes.
4. Grill the chicken for 5–7 minutes per side, or until fully cooked and the internal temperature reaches 165°F (75°C).
5. Serve immediately.

Lemon Fluff Pie

Ingredients:

- 1 cup heavy cream
- 1/2 cup cream cheese, softened
- 1/4 cup erythritol (or sweetener of choice)
- 2 tbsp fresh lemon juice
- 1 tbsp lemon zest
- 1 tsp vanilla extract
- 1/2 cup almond flour (for crust)
- 1/4 cup butter, melted

Instructions:

1. Preheat oven to 350°F (175°C).
2. For the crust, combine almond flour and melted butter, and press into the bottom of a pie dish. Bake for 10–12 minutes until golden.
3. In a bowl, whisk together heavy cream, cream cheese, erythritol, lemon juice, lemon zest, and vanilla extract until smooth and fluffy.
4. Pour the mixture into the cooled crust and chill for at least 2 hours.
5. Serve chilled.

Lemon Maple Roasted Carrots

Ingredients:

- 1 lb baby carrots
- 2 tbsp olive oil
- 1 tbsp fresh lemon juice
- 1 tbsp maple extract (or a few drops of liquid stevia for keto)
- Salt and pepper to taste

Instructions:

1. Preheat oven to 400°F (200°C).
2. In a bowl, toss the carrots with olive oil, lemon juice, maple extract, salt, and pepper.
3. Arrange the carrots on a baking sheet in a single layer.
4. Roast for 20–25 minutes, or until tender and caramelized.
5. Serve hot.

Lemon Scones

Ingredients:

- 2 cups almond flour
- 1/4 cup erythritol (or sweetener of choice)
- 1 tsp baking powder
- 1/4 tsp salt
- 2 tbsp butter, cold and cubed
- 1/4 cup heavy cream
- 1 large egg
- 1 tbsp fresh lemon juice
- 1 tsp lemon zest

Instructions:

1. Preheat oven to 350°F (175°C).
2. In a bowl, mix almond flour, erythritol, baking powder, and salt.
3. Add cold butter and cut it into the dry ingredients using a pastry cutter or fork until the mixture resembles coarse crumbs.
4. In a separate bowl, whisk together heavy cream, egg, lemon juice, and lemon zest.
5. Add the wet ingredients to the dry mixture and stir until combined.
6. Shape the dough into a round disk and slice into 8 wedges.

7. Place the wedges on a baking sheet and bake for 12–15 minutes, or until golden.

8. Serve warm.

Lemon Lush Dessert

Ingredients:

- 2 cups almond flour
- 1/4 cup butter, melted
- 2 tbsp erythritol (or sweetener of choice)
- 8 oz cream cheese, softened
- 1/2 cup heavy cream
- 1/4 cup lemon juice
- 1 tbsp lemon zest
- 2 tbsp powdered erythritol (for topping)

Instructions:

1. Preheat oven to 350°F (175°C).
2. Combine almond flour, melted butter, and erythritol to form a crust. Press it into the bottom of a 9x9 baking dish and bake for 10 minutes.
3. In a bowl, beat the cream cheese, heavy cream, lemon juice, and lemon zest until smooth and fluffy.
4. Spread the cream cheese mixture over the cooled crust.
5. Refrigerate for at least 2 hours to set.
6. Sprinkle powdered erythritol on top before serving.

Lemon-Cucumber Salad

Ingredients:

- 1 cucumber, thinly sliced
- 1 tbsp fresh lemon juice
- 1 tsp lemon zest
- 2 tbsp olive oil
- 1/2 tsp salt
- 1/4 tsp black pepper
- Fresh dill or parsley for garnish

Instructions:

1. In a bowl, combine cucumber slices with lemon juice, lemon zest, olive oil, salt, and pepper.
2. Toss gently until well mixed.
3. Garnish with fresh dill or parsley.
4. Serve chilled as a refreshing side dish.

Lemon Shrimp Scampi

Ingredients:

- 1 lb large shrimp, peeled and deveined
- 2 tbsp olive oil
- 4 cloves garlic, minced
- 2 tbsp fresh lemon juice
- 1 tsp lemon zest
- 1/4 cup dry white wine (optional)
- Salt and pepper to taste
- Fresh parsley for garnish

Instructions:

1. Heat olive oil in a large skillet over medium-high heat.
2. Add garlic and cook for 1–2 minutes, until fragrant.
3. Add shrimp, lemon juice, lemon zest, wine (if using), salt, and pepper. Cook for 3–4 minutes, until shrimp turn pink and are cooked through.
4. Garnish with fresh parsley and serve immediately.

Lemon Baked Cod

Ingredients:

- 4 cod fillets
- 2 tbsp olive oil
- 2 tbsp fresh lemon juice
- 1 tsp lemon zest
- 2 cloves garlic, minced
- Salt and pepper to taste
- Fresh parsley for garnish

Instructions:

1. Preheat oven to 375°F (190°C).
2. Place cod fillets on a baking sheet lined with parchment paper.
3. Drizzle olive oil, lemon juice, lemon zest, and garlic over the fillets.
4. Season with salt and pepper.
5. Bake for 12–15 minutes, until the cod flakes easily with a fork.
6. Garnish with fresh parsley before serving.

Lemon Almond Cake

Ingredients:

- 2 cups almond flour
- 1/4 cup erythritol (or sweetener of choice)
- 1 tsp baking powder
- 1/4 tsp salt
- 1/4 cup butter, softened
- 3 large eggs
- 1/4 cup lemon juice
- 2 tbsp lemon zest
- 1 tsp vanilla extract
- 1/4 cup unsweetened almond milk

Instructions:

1. Preheat oven to 350°F (175°C).
2. Grease an 8-inch round cake pan.
3. In a bowl, combine almond flour, erythritol, baking powder, and salt.
4. In another bowl, whisk together butter, eggs, lemon juice, lemon zest, vanilla, and almond milk.
5. Stir the wet ingredients into the dry ingredients until smooth.

6. Pour the batter into the prepared pan and bake for 25–30 minutes, or until a toothpick comes out clean.

7. Let the cake cool before serving.

Lemon-Infused Olive Oil Pasta

Ingredients:

- 2 cups zucchini noodles (or shirataki noodles for lower carb)
- 2 tbsp olive oil
- 2 tbsp fresh lemon juice
- 1 tsp lemon zest
- 2 cloves garlic, minced
- Salt and pepper to taste
- Fresh basil or parsley for garnish

Instructions:

1. Heat olive oil in a skillet over medium heat.
2. Add garlic and cook for 1–2 minutes until fragrant.
3. Add zucchini noodles and sauté for 3–4 minutes, until tender.
4. Stir in lemon juice, lemon zest, salt, and pepper.
5. Cook for an additional 1–2 minutes, then garnish with fresh basil or parsley.
6. Serve immediately.

Lemon Glazed Donuts

Ingredients:

- 2 cups almond flour
- 1/4 cup erythritol (or sweetener of choice)
- 1 tsp baking powder
- 1/4 tsp salt
- 2 large eggs
- 1/4 cup unsweetened almond milk
- 1/4 cup butter, melted
- 2 tbsp fresh lemon juice
- 1 tsp lemon zest

For Glaze:

- 1/2 cup powdered erythritol
- 2 tbsp fresh lemon juice
- 1 tbsp almond milk

Instructions:

1. Preheat oven to 350°F (175°C) and grease a donut pan.
2. In a bowl, combine almond flour, erythritol, baking powder, and salt.

3. In another bowl, whisk together eggs, almond milk, melted butter, lemon juice, and lemon zest.

4. Stir the wet ingredients into the dry ingredients until smooth.

5. Pour the batter into the donut pan and bake for 12–15 minutes, or until golden brown and a toothpick comes out clean.

6. In a small bowl, mix powdered erythritol, lemon juice, and almond milk to make the glaze.

7. Drizzle the glaze over the donuts before serving.

Lemon Zest Vinaigrette

Ingredients:

- 1/4 cup fresh lemon juice
- 1 tbsp lemon zest
- 1/2 cup olive oil
- 1 tbsp Dijon mustard
- 1 tsp honey (optional, or use a keto sweetener)
- Salt and pepper to taste
- 1 clove garlic, minced

Instructions:

1. In a small bowl or jar, combine lemon juice, lemon zest, mustard, honey, garlic, salt, and pepper.
2. Slowly whisk in the olive oil until the dressing is emulsified.
3. Store in the fridge for up to a week.
4. Drizzle over salads and enjoy!

Lemon Chia Seed Pudding

Ingredients:

- 1 cup unsweetened almond milk
- 2 tbsp chia seeds
- 1 tbsp fresh lemon juice
- 1 tsp lemon zest
- 1-2 tbsp erythritol or your preferred sweetener

Instructions:

1. In a bowl, whisk together almond milk, lemon juice, lemon zest, sweetener, and chia seeds.
2. Let sit for 5 minutes, then stir again to prevent clumping.
3. Cover and refrigerate for at least 2 hours, or overnight, until the chia seeds expand and the pudding thickens.
4. Stir before serving, and garnish with extra lemon zest or berries if desired.

Lemon Tofu Stir Fry

Ingredients:

- 1 block firm tofu, pressed and cubed
- 2 tbsp olive oil
- 1 tbsp soy sauce or coconut aminos
- 2 tbsp fresh lemon juice
- 1 tsp lemon zest
- 2 cloves garlic, minced
- 1 bell pepper, sliced
- 1 cup broccoli florets
- Salt and pepper to taste

Instructions:

1. In a large skillet, heat olive oil over medium heat.
2. Add cubed tofu and cook until golden on all sides. Remove from the skillet and set aside.
3. In the same skillet, add garlic and cook for 1 minute until fragrant.
4. Add bell pepper and broccoli, stir-frying for 4–5 minutes until tender-crisp.
5. Add tofu back to the pan, then stir in soy sauce, lemon juice, lemon zest, salt, and pepper.
6. Cook for another 2 minutes, tossing to combine. Serve warm.

Lemon-Blueberry Muffins

Ingredients:

- 2 cups almond flour
- 1/4 cup erythritol (or sweetener of choice)
- 1 tsp baking powder
- 1/4 tsp salt
- 2 large eggs
- 1/4 cup unsweetened almond milk
- 1/4 cup melted butter
- 1/4 cup fresh lemon juice
- 1 tbsp lemon zest
- 1/2 cup fresh or frozen blueberries

Instructions:

1. Preheat oven to 350°F (175°C) and line a muffin tin with paper liners.
2. In a bowl, mix almond flour, erythritol, baking powder, and salt.
3. In another bowl, whisk together eggs, almond milk, melted butter, lemon juice, and lemon zest.
4. Add wet ingredients to dry ingredients and mix until just combined.
5. Gently fold in blueberries.

6. Spoon the batter into muffin tins and bake for 18–20 minutes, or until a toothpick comes out clean.

7. Let cool before serving.

Lemon-Poppy Seed Cake

Ingredients:

- 2 cups almond flour
- 1/2 cup erythritol (or sweetener of choice)
- 1 tsp baking powder
- 1/4 tsp salt
- 4 large eggs
- 1/4 cup unsweetened almond milk
- 1/4 cup melted butter
- 2 tbsp fresh lemon juice
- 1 tbsp lemon zest
- 2 tbsp poppy seeds
- 1 tsp vanilla extract

Instructions:

1. Preheat oven to 350°F (175°C). Grease a loaf pan or cake pan.
2. In a bowl, combine almond flour, erythritol, baking powder, salt, and poppy seeds.
3. In another bowl, whisk together eggs, almond milk, melted butter, lemon juice, lemon zest, and vanilla extract.
4. Add the wet ingredients to the dry ingredients and mix until smooth.

5. Pour the batter into the prepared pan and bake for 30–35 minutes, or until a toothpick comes out clean.

6. Let cool before serving.

Lemon Rosemary Roasted Chicken

Ingredients:

- 4 bone-in, skin-on chicken thighs
- 2 tbsp olive oil
- 2 tbsp fresh lemon juice
- 1 tbsp lemon zest
- 2 tbsp fresh rosemary, chopped
- 4 cloves garlic, minced
- Salt and pepper to taste

Instructions:

1. Preheat oven to 375°F (190°C).
2. In a bowl, mix olive oil, lemon juice, lemon zest, rosemary, garlic, salt, and pepper.
3. Rub the mixture all over the chicken thighs.
4. Place the chicken on a baking sheet and roast for 35–40 minutes, or until the internal temperature reaches 165°F (75°C).
5. Let rest for a few minutes before serving.

Lemon Watermelon Salad

Ingredients:

- 4 cups cubed watermelon
- 1 tbsp fresh lemon juice
- 1 tsp lemon zest
- 1 tbsp mint, finely chopped
- 1 tbsp feta cheese, crumbled (optional)
- Salt to taste

Instructions:

1. In a large bowl, combine watermelon, lemon juice, lemon zest, and mint.
2. Gently toss to combine.
3. If using, sprinkle feta cheese over the salad.
4. Season with a pinch of salt to enhance the flavors.
5. Serve chilled as a refreshing summer side dish.